Accounting for Hedge Funds

Steven M. Bragg

AccountingTools®

ISBN-13: 978-1-64221-133-7

For more information about AccountingTools® products, visit our Web site at www.accountingtools.com.

Table of Contents

About the Author

Steven Bragg, CPA, has been the chief financial officer or controller of four companies, as well as a consulting manager at Ernst & Young. He received a master's degree in finance from Bentley College, an MBA from Babson College, and a Bachelor's degree in Economics from the University of Maine. He has been a two-time president of the Colorado Mountain Club, and is an avid alpine skier, mountain biker, and certified master diver. Mr. Bragg resides in Centennial, Colorado. He has written more than 300 books and courses, including *New Controller Guidebook*, *GAAP Guidebook*, and *Payroll Management*.

Steven maintains the accountingtools.com web site, which contains continuing professional education courses, the Accounting Best Practices podcast, and thousands of articles on accounting subjects.

Buy Additional AccountingTools Courses

AccountingTools offers more than 1,500 hours of CPE courses, with concentrations in accounting, auditing, finance, taxation, and ethics. Related courses that you might like include:

- Accounting for Derivatives and Hedges
- Accounting for Investment Companies
- Accounting for Investments

Go to accountingtools.com/cpe to view these additional courses.

AccountingTools®

Accounting for Hedge Funds

Introduction

This booklet covers what hedge funds do, their fee structure, and the essentials of their accounting operations. It addresses the accounting for a hedge fund's portfolio, investor transactions, side pocket investments, and the main types of expenses. It also deals with the concept of net asset value and how to verify it through an ongoing reconciliation process. In short, the booklet is designed to give the reader an understanding of the basic accounting functions within a hedge fund.

Overview of Hedge Funds

A hedge fund pools the money of contributing investors and tries to achieve above-market returns through a wide variety of investment strategies. Hedge funds do not necessarily subscribe to a particular investment philosophy, so they can roam the investment landscape, looking for anomalies of all types to take advantage of. However, they usually develop investment strategies that are designed to generate gains, irrespective of movements in the stock market, either up or down. This approach of always seeking a positive return, irrespective of market conditions, is called the *absolute return strategy*.

Hedge fund investment strategies may include the following:

- *Leverage*. There may be a considerable quantity of leverage (that is, investing borrowed funds) to achieve outsized returns on a relatively small capital base.
- *Short sales*. Hedge funds may borrow shares and sell them, in the expectation that the price of a security will drop, after which they buy the securities on the open market and return the borrowed securities. This is a very risky strategy, since a share price increase can introduce potentially unlimited losses.
- *Derivatives*. Investments are made in any number of derivatives, which can pay off based on a vast number of possible underlying indices or other measures.

Because of the enhanced use of leverage, as well as other speculative strategies, there is some probability of loss in a hedge fund. The level of potential loss for an investor is accentuated by the common requirement that investments cannot be withdrawn from a hedge fund for a period of at least one year. This requirement allows a hedge fund manager to employ longer-term investment strategies. Alternatively, withdrawals within a shorter period may be allowed, but only if a significant penalty is paid. This requirement is needed because some hedge fund investments cannot be easily liquidated to meet a cash withdrawal demand by an investor.

Hedge funds typically do not accept small investments, with minimum contributions starting as high as $1 million. Hedge fund managers are compensated with a percentage of the total assets in the investment pool, as well as a percentage of all profits generated. For example, a fund manager could take from 1% to 2% of all capital under management, as well as 20% of all profits earned. The management fee covers the administration of the fund, while the bonus provides a performance incentive for the fund manager. The management fee is based on the net assets of the fund, and is usually paid out in advance, on a quarterly basis. The incentive fee is usually calculated on a quarterly basis, and is paid out to the fund manager once a year.

Hedge funds may be organized as limited partnerships or limited liability companies, where there is a general manager who runs the fund (and acts as the money manager) and a group of investors who are all limited partners. Each limited partner has an economic interest in the entity that equals the amount of their investment, and they share in any resulting gains and losses based on their economic interest. Because of the liability structure of these organizations, investor losses are capped at the amount they invest; they are not liable for any additional losses incurred by the fund.

> **Note:** The term "hedge" in the name "hedge fund" is a misnomer, since it seems to imply that a fund attempts to mitigate its risk. This term comes from the early days of hedge funds, when funds attempted to reduce the risk of securities price declines in a bear market by shorting securities. Nowadays, the pursuit of outsized returns is the primary goal, and that cannot usually be achieved while risk is also being hedged.

There are three types of hedge fund clients. Domestic taxable investors are investors who are required to pay taxes on any income earned from their investments. These investors are typically for-profit entities based in the United States, or individual investors. Domestic non-taxable investors have a non-taxable tax status, such as pension plans, charitable foundations, and trusts. Finally, non-taxable offshore investors are any parties not located in the United States, and who therefore have no obligation to pay taxes to the Internal Revenue Service. Domestic non-taxable investors and non-taxable offshore investors will usually want to invest in an offshore fund structured as a corporation, because the government would otherwise tax them on any investments made in onshore funds; instead, they are merely making a passive investment in an entity that invests in the financial markets.

Hedge Fund Service Providers

A hedge fund does not conduct operations in a vacuum. Instead, it works with a group of service providers who handle certain aspects of its business. Doing so allows the fund's employees to concentrate on the execution of their investment strategies. These outside parties are specialists that have the necessary infrastructure and knowledge base to handle certain issues more efficiently and effectively than a hedge fund could with its own staff. The most important hedge fund service providers are as follows:

- *Prime broker*. Provides real-time trade execution, portfolio reporting, risk management, and securities lending services to the hedge fund, as well as office space and technology support.
- *Administrator*. Keeps the accounting records for the fund, tracks asset flows, develops portfolio valuations, operates anti-money laundering procedures, and prepares investor reports. It is essentially an external accounting department. This is a cost-effective solution for smaller funds.
- *Attorney*. Sets up the entity structure for the business, an offering memorandum to issue to investors, and a subscription agreement. The offering memorandum describes what the fund does, how it invests, and its fee structure. The subscription agreement is a form that investors complete when they want to invest in the fund, requiring them to make a variety of declarations about their financial health, investing knowledge, and investment objectives.
- *Audit firm*. Advises on accounting issues, tax liabilities, and fund reporting, and conducts an annual audit of a fund's accounts.

Net Asset Value

Net asset value (NAV) is the net value of a fund. It has multiple uses, which are noted in the following bullet points:

- *Entry price*. Net asset value is used to price new investors buying into the fund.
- *Exit price*. Net asset value is used to price the redemptions paid out to investors leaving the fund.
- *Performance reporting*. Net asset value is periodically reported to all fund investors. Some investors demand that the NAV be calculated and reported on a daily basis.
- *Fee calculations*. Net asset value may be a component of the calculation used to derive management fees and incentive fees that are payable to the fund manager.

Net asset value is calculated as the total value of a hedge fund's assets minus the total value of its liabilities. A fund's assets include cash, securities, receivables, and other investments, while its liabilities include its accounts payable and debt. The most accurate NAV is derived under the accrual basis of accounting, where expenses and liabilities are recorded as soon as they are incurred, rather than when cash is paid.

Exactly how a fund's NAV is calculated should be stated in detail in its offering memorandum as a separately-stated valuation policy, so that investors understand how the calculation is conducted before they invest in the fund.

Net asset value is based on the *mark to market* concept, which involves adjusting the value of an asset to reflect its value as determined by current market conditions. The market value is determined based on what a hedge fund would receive for an asset if it were to be sold on the current date. This concept is applied to the valuation of actively traded securities, since market information is readily available for them. The valuation policy usually states that these securities are to be valued at the market price at the close of trading.

The simplest scenario for calculating a NAV at the end of each day arises when a fund only invests in one market and in one type of investment. For example, when all investments are made through the New York Stock Exchange, one can simply price all investments at the close, which is at 4 p.m.

Determining a fund's NAV is more difficult when its investments are spread across multiple markets around the world. In this scenario, markets close at different times of the day, so a NAV calculation is based on a rolling set of closing times. Since many assets are being constantly traded around the world, when is it possible to call a halt and calculate net asset value? One approach to a NAV calculation is to gradually compile values at the closing time of each successive relevant market. The NAV is then calculated as the sum of the prices at each market's close. The following exhibit contains an example of this approach, where a hedge fund has investments in a number of markets.

Sample Multi-Market NAV Calculation

Exchange	Closing Time (Eastern Time)	Value at Closing
Tokyo Stock Exchange	1:00 a.m.	$2,300
London Stock Exchange	10:30 a.m.	3,700
New York Stock Exchange	4:00 p.m.	800
Chicago Board of Trade	4:15 p.m.	-1,100
Net asset value		$5,700

The valuation task is more difficult for over-the-counter securities. These securities trade through a less formal trading system, and so it can be difficult to obtain current market prices. In these cases, the fund's valuation policy should specify an alternative valuation method, such as valuing securities based on a basket of similar securities, or perhaps by using a valuation model.

> **Note:** The valuation policy should state the primary source of market price information, as well as a secondary source. The policy can also state whether the primary and secondary sources are to be cross-checked against each other for pricing anomalies, and what to do when such anomalies are found. The policy may mandate a review process when there are major price movements that exceed a certain trigger point.

The nature of the fund's legal structure drives how NAV is calculated. If it is structured as a partnership, then the calculation results in gains and losses being allocated to the individual partner accounts. If the fund has instead been set up as a corporation (as is common with an offshore fund), then the NAV is divided by the total number of shares issued to arrive at a net asset value per share.

EXAMPLE

The Beach Fund is set up as a Grand Cayman corporation. At the end of the month, the fund's NAV is calculated as $580 million. The fund has issued 3,135,135 shares, which results in a NAV per share of $185.

The accountant must follow a rigid procedure to ensure that a fund's NAV has been correctly calculated. Key issues to address are as follows:

- *Accounting period.* All transactions must be recorded within the correct accounting period. This means that all investment transactions should be recorded as of their trade date, and that all expenses and fees charged should be accrued within the correct period. Similarly, interest income should be accrued on a daily basis.
- *Asset and liability inclusions.* Ensure that all assets are included in the NAV calculation, including investments, amounts due from the prime broker, dividend income receivable, and interest income receivable. Similarly, one should ensure that all liabilities are included in the calculation, including amounts payable to the prime broker, management fees payable, incentive fees payable, and fund expenses payable.
- *Valuation policy.* All assets in the fund's portfolio should be valued in accordance with its valuation policy, with no exceptions.

The Net Asset Value Reconciliation

Net asset value is *the* essential measurement in a hedge fund, so it is essential to conduct a reconciliation process to ensure that the values used are correct, and that all transactions have been included. A formal reconciliation process should be used for every account, such as cash, investments, receivables, and both realized and unrealized gains and losses.

Most accountants will be familiar with the cash reconciliation process, where the cash book balance is compared to the balance in the prime broker's cash accounts for the fund. For example, the cash balance per the fund's books is $82,000, while the balance in the fund's prime broker account is $71,000. The difference of $11,000 is due to unsettled trades and late trades, which are classified in the reconciliation as such. Other possible reconciling items are dividend payments, subscriptions, redemptions, and cancelled trades.

The same process must be conducted for a hedge fund's security positions, reconciling the ending balances on the fund's books to those of its prime broker. This reconciliation must be conducted both for the number of units held and the market value by security.

EXAMPLE

The Hedgehog Fund has on its books 5,000 shares of a company with stock ticker symbol AAA (Amalgamated American Accountants), with a market value of $190,000 (at a market price of $38/share). However, according to the fund's broker holding report, the fund only has 4,500 shares with a market value of $166,500 (at a market value of $37/share).

Upon investigation, the fund's accountant finds that there is an unsettled trade causing the difference. Hedgehog had purchased an additional 500 shares of AAA stock, which has yet to settle on the books of the prime broker. She found this difference by reviewing the fund's open trades to see if any of them match the unit variance. In addition, she finds that the prime broker has been valuing the shares with a different source than the one used by Hedgehog. She locates this difference by reviewing the share price information on Hedgehog's secondary source of market data (which is the primary source used by the prime broker).

A reconciliation should also be conducted on the fund's income accounts to see if accrued dividends and interest income match actual cash receipts. Variable rate securities are a particular source of reconciliation problems, due to interest rate changes that have not been incorporated into the fund's security master file. Also, when interest income is being accrued each day, minor variances from the actual interest amounts paid are likely to crop up, typically requiring a minor adjustment to the interest income account balances.

A final reconciliation area is the fund's expenses. The accountant should compare the fees being charged by the prime broker to the fund's broker agreement with it, to ensure that fees are being charged correctly. Also, if the accountant has been accruing certain expenses, the reconciliation should determine whether actual cash payments match the accrued expense totals. This is also a good time to implement an approval control, which is to ensure that an authorized manager has reviewed and approved all significant expenses.

Accounting for the Portfolio

The entire asset base of a hedge fund is its portfolio. Therefore, in order to derive a fund's NAV, the accountant must have a firm grasp of how to account for asset acquisitions and dispositions, as well as the asset changes that can occur while these assets are being held, including dividend income, interest income, and unrealized gains and losses on assets held. The assets that a hedge fund is most likely to hold are equities and bonds. We will describe the accounting for each of these elements of a portfolio in the following sub-sections.

Equities

Depending on its investment strategy, a hedge fund may elect to invest heavily in equity securities. The fund's trading activity may include common stock, preferred stock, stock warrants, and rights. The characteristics of these equity types are as follows:

- *Common stock.* This is an ownership share in a corporation that allows its holders voting rights at shareholder meetings, as well as the opportunity to receive dividends. If the corporation liquidates, then common stockholders receive their share of the proceeds of the liquidation after all creditors and preferred stockholders have been paid.
- *Preferred stock.* This is a class of equity ownership that has a more senior claim on the earnings and assets of a business than common stock. In the event of liquidation, the holders of preferred stock must be paid off before common stockholders, but after secured debt holders. Preferred stock also pays a dividend; this payment is usually cumulative, so any delayed prior payments must also be paid before distributions can be made to the holders of company stock.
- *Stock warrants.* This instrument gives its holder the right, but not the obligation, to purchase a certain number of a company's shares at a pre-determined price, within a defined time period. Warrants do not give their holder the right to receive dividends, and have no voting rights.
- *Stock rights.* This instrument gives its holder the right, but not the obligation, to buy the shares of a company at a specific exercise price for a designated period of time. It is generally used to give current shareholders the right to buy additional shares as part of the issuer's next stock sale.

Equity transactions are accounted for as of the *trade date*, which is the date when an order related to a security is executed in the market. When an order is placed very late in a trading day, execution may be delayed to the next day; this means that the trade date is the following business day. Thus, when a fund manager acquires equity securities, the initial entry is as follows (assuming a $10,000 investment):

	Debit	Credit
Equities (asset)	$10,000	
Due to broker (liability)		$10,000

Once the securities are transferred into the fund's account on the settlement date, the fund pays the broker, as noted in the following journal entry. The settlement date is the date when a trade is finalized.

The settlement date for stocks and bonds is usually two business days after the execution date, while it is the next business day for government securities and options.

	Debit	Credit
Due to broker (liability)	$10,000	
Cash (asset)		$10,000

When equity is sold, the accountant clears the asset from the fund's books and records a receivable due from the broker, as well as any gain or loss. A sample entry follows, which assumes that the $10,000 equity investment was sold for a gain of $200.

	Debit	Credit
Due from broker (asset)	$10,200	
Equities (asset)		$10,000
Realized gain on equities (revenue)		200

If the fund had instead sold the equity at a $200 loss, the corresponding entry would have been as follows:

	Debit	Credit
Due from broker (asset)	$9,800	
Realized loss on equities (loss)	200	
Equities (asset)		$10,000

The fund manager might elect to sell a stock short, in which the manager is speculating on a decline in the price of the stock. It involves borrowing the stock of a company with an expectation of earning a profit later, when the fund can buy back the stock at a lower price. The basic short selling process is as follows:

1. Set up a margin account at a brokerage firm, where the hedge fund uses the value of its investments placed with the brokerage firm to borrow money.
2. Place a short sale transaction with the brokerage firm. The hedge fund is borrowing the target company's stock from the broker. The broker, in turn, is borrowing the shares either from its own inventory, or from another brokerage firm, or the account of another client. The hedge fund then sells the shares, pocketing what it hopes will be the highest price at which the shares will sell.
3. Wait for the stock price to (hopefully) decline, and then buy a matching number of shares on the open market to close out the transaction, returning the shares to the brokerage.

Short selling is a risky activity. For example, if a company's stock sells for $5 and its price drops all the way to zero, then a short seller can earn a maximum of

$5. However, if the price increases to $100, then the short seller has just lost $95. Thus, there is a limited upside potential and a massive downside potential for a short seller.

EXAMPLE

The manager of the Hedgehog Fund believes that the price of Eskimo Construction's common stock is too high, at $28. Accordingly, the fund borrows 1,000 shares of Eskimo common stock from its broker and sells it at the prevailing $28 price. Two weeks later, the price of the stock has fallen to $25, at which point Hedgehog buys 1,000 shares at $25 and returns the shares to the brokerage, having pocketed a $3,000 gain.

When accounting for a short position, the fund is incurring a liability, since it owes the brokerage the amount that it has borrowed. Once the shares are repurchased on the open market and returned to the brokerage, then the obligation is settled.

Dividend Income

A dividend is a payment to shareholders of a portion of a corporation's earnings. Dividends are typically paid on a recurring quarterly or annual basis, though a firm's board of directors may occasionally vote to issue a one-time dividend to distribute excess cash for which the business has no internal need. Conversely, dividends are paid at a fixed rate to the holders of a company's preferred stock.

The accountant initially records a dividend receivable when it is first announced by the issuing company. This occurs on the *ex-dividend date*, which is the date on which it is determined who will receive a company's dividend. For this to take place, a hedge fund must be holding the stock on the ex-dividend date.

EXAMPLE

ABC Company declares a $1 dividend, payable to shareholders of record on January 11. The ex-dividend date is January 9. Several scenarios are:

- The Hedgehog Fund buys 10 shares of ABC Company on January 8, and sells them on January 9. Hedgehog is entitled to the $1 dividend on each of the shares, since it was the last owner of record prior to the ex-dividend date.
- The Hedgehog Fund has held 500 shares of ABC Company stock for the last three years, and retains its ownership through the ex-dividend date. Hedgehog is entitled to the $1 dividend on each of the 500 shares.
- The Hedgehog Fund buys 250 shares of ABC Company on January 10. This is after the ex-dividend date, so it is not entitled to the declared dividend.

As an example of the accounting for a dividend, a hedge fund is notified of a $3 dividend on each of the 1,000 shares it holds. On the ex-dividend date, the accountant records the following entry:

	Debit	Credit
Dividends receivable (asset)	$3,000	
Dividend income (revenue)		$3,000

On the dividend payment date, the accountant records the following entry:

	Debit	Credit
Cash (asset)	$3,000	
Dividends receivable (asset)		$3,000

Note: Since the ex-dividend date is the first date on which a dividend appears on the books of a hedge fund, this is the first date on which it impacts the net asset value calculation for the fund.

Bonds

Depending on its investment strategy, a hedge fund may elect to invest heavily in bonds. A *bond* is a fixed obligation to pay that is issued by a corporation or government entity to investors. Bonds usually include a periodic coupon payment and are paid off as of a specific maturity date. A fund may acquire bonds at par (their stated value), at a discount from their stated value, or at a premium over their stated value. A bond is acquired at a discount when its stated interest rate is lower than the market interest rate, so that the price paid results in an effective interest rate that matches the market rate. Similarly, a bond is acquired at a premium when its stated interest rate is higher than the market rate, also resulting in an effective interest rate that matches the market rate.

There are many types of bonds. The following list represents a sampling of the more common types:

- *Convertible bond.* This bond can be converted into the common stock of the issuer at a predetermined conversion ratio.
- *Debenture.* This bond has no collateral associated with it. A variation is the subordinated debenture, which has junior rights to collateral.
- *Deferred interest bond.* This bond offers little or no interest at the start of the bond term, and more interest near the end. The format is useful for businesses currently having little cash with which to pay interest.
- *Guaranteed bond.* The payments associated with this bond are guaranteed by a third party, which can result in a lower effective interest rate for the issuer.
- *Income bond.* The issuer is only obligated to make interest payments to bond holders if the issuer or a specific project earns a profit. If the bond terms allow

for cumulative interest, then the unpaid interest will accumulate until such time as there is sufficient income to pay the amounts owed.

- *Mortgage bond.* This bond is backed by real estate or equipment owned by the issuer.
- *Serial bond.* This bond is gradually paid off in each successive year, so the total amount of debt outstanding is gradually reduced.
- *Variable rate bond.* The interest rate paid on this bond varies with a benchmark, such as a bank's prime rate.
- *Zero coupon bond.* No interest is paid on this type of bond. Instead, investors buy the bonds at large discounts to their face values in order to earn an effective interest rate.

When a hedge fund buys a bond, the accountant records the following initial entry on the trade date (assuming a $1,000 purchase):

	Debit	Credit
Bonds (asset)	$1,000	
Due to broker (liability)		$1,000

On the settlement date, the hedge fund pays the broker, which the accountant records with the following entry:

	Debit	Credit
Due to broker (liability)	$1,000	
Cash (asset)		$1,000

When a bond is sold, the accountant clears the asset from the fund's books and records a receivable due from the broker, as well as any gain or loss. A sample entry follows which assumes that the $1,000 bond was sold for a gain of $100.

	Debit	Credit
Due from broker (asset)	$1,100	
Bonds (asset)		$1,000
Realized gain on bonds (revenue)		100

If the fund had instead sold the bond at a $100 loss, the corresponding entry would have been as follows:

	Debit	Credit
Due from broker (asset)	$900	
Realized loss on bonds (loss)	100	
Bonds (asset)		$1,000

Bond prices are expressed as a percentage of par. Therefore, in order to determine whether a gain or loss has been realized from the sale of a bond, one must multiply its par value by its price. For example, if a bond has a par value of $1,000 and is currently priced at 98.25, then the value of the bond is $982.50.

Interest Income

A hedge fund accrues the interest on its bond holdings on a daily basis. For example, if the accrued daily interest income on a fund's bond holdings is $650, then the associated entry would be:

	Debit	Credit
Accrued interest on bonds (asset)	$650	
Bond interest income (revenue)		$650

The accrued interest total is then converted into a receivable on the date when bond interest is due, as noted in the following entry:

	Debit	Credit
Interest receivable (asset)	$650	
Accrued interest on bonds (asset)		$650

Once the interest payment is received, the receivable is eliminated and replaced by cash, as noted in the following entry:

	Debit	Credit
Cash (asset)	$650	
Interest receivable (asset)		$650

The amount of accrued interest may be slightly off from the amount actually received, due to calculation differences; if so, the accrued interest balance should be adjusted to match the amount received.

The same daily interest accrual should be used for shorter-term investments, such as commercial paper and certificates of deposit.

Accounting for Investor Transactions

Since many hedge funds are structured as partnerships, they should maintain a capital account for each investor. Each capital account tracks all activity related to the relevant investor. The information in the capital accounts should be summarized and periodically reported to the fund investors. Possible activities recorded in this account are noted in the following exhibit.

Investor Account Transaction Types

Transaction Type	Description
+ Subscriptions	When investors put money into the fund
+ Income allocations	When the fund earnings are allocated to investors
- Loss allocations	When fund losses are allocated to investors
- Incentive fee allocations	When the fund manager's incentive fee is allocated to investors
- Management fee allocations	When the fund manager's management fee is allocated to investors
- Redemptions	When investors withdraw money from the fund

When a fund has realized profits or losses on its investments through the sale of assets, it has two available methods for allocating them to the fund partners. When using the *layering method*, these profits and losses are allocated to the partner accounts as of the date when they were realized. An alternative is the *aggregate method*, under which all realized profits and losses are netted and then allocated to partners. The aggregate method is less complex and therefore more efficient, and should generate approximately the same results as the layering method, and so is recommended.

When a hedge fund is instead structured as a corporation, it issues shares to investors when they make an investment in the fund. The number of shares issued will be priced at the NAV on the day of the investment.

When redemptions are made from a fund, the departing investor may be forced to wait for payment, due to any lock-up provisions imposed by the fund that mandate a minimum holding period. When a redemption is demanded within a shorter time frame, the fund may subtract an exit fee from the redemption payment, along with any subtractions for management fees and incentive fees.

Side Pocket Investments

A *side pocket* is a type of account that a hedge fund uses to segregate riskier or illiquid assets from the rest of its investments. Examples of the assets that may be recorded in this account are antiques, delisted stocks, over-the-counter stocks, private equity investments, and trade claims[1]. Typically, once an investment is recorded in a side

---

[1] Trade claims are claims by creditors (typically suppliers) against bankrupt businesses; it is exceedingly difficult to obtain prices for these assets.

pocket account, only the fund's current participants are entitled to a share of it. Any investors entering the fund at a later date will not receive a share of the proceeds from these assets.

The investments recorded in a side pocket account are fully recorded in the accounting records of a hedge fund, but they are tracked separately from more mainstream assets. A key issue is how they are valued, since it may be difficult to arrive at a fair market value for them. To ensure that there is no conflict with investors over the valuation methodology used, the valuation approach to be employed should be clearly stated in the offering memorandum.

When a side pocket account is created, each investor receives a pro rata share of the fund's investment in the account. When investors leave the fund, they may not be able to redeem their side pocket investment right away. Instead, they will receive a share of the value when assets in the account are either liquidated or relocated to the general fund. By separating side-pocket assets from redemptions, the fund manager can hold illiquid assets for a longer period of time, so that some asset appreciation can be experienced.

Accounting for Expenses

The bulk of the fees incurred by a hedge fund will be charged to it by the service providers noted earlier – its administrator, auditors, attorney, and prime broker – with the bulk of the fees coming from the prime broker. This is especially the case when the hedge fund staff is renting space on the premises of the prime broker. Otherwise, a fifth expense area will be the cost to maintain office space, along with utilities, office supplies, and so forth. The administrator will charge a minimum fixed amount, irrespective of fund performance, and may charge an additional fee that slides up or down based on the NAV level.

The accountant will be called upon to keep close track of expenses, as noted earlier in the Net Asset Value Reconciliation section. Since expenses reduce net asset value, and investors want to see as high a NAV as possible, there is continuing downward pressure on expenses – perhaps more so than in most industries.

As noted earlier, the hedge fund manager is paid a management fee that is generally in the range of 1-2% of the assets under management, as well as an incentive fee that is only paid out if the manager can boost the asset value above a previous highwater mark.

A fund manager's incentive fee is based on the *high-water mark*, which is the fund value baseline from which any gains are calculated – and from which the manager's incentive fee is derived. The use of a high-water mark means that a fund manager will only receive an incentive fee if the value of the fund's portfolio exceeds the greatest value that it had previously achieved. If the value of the portfolio subsequently drops, then the fund manager must bring its value back to the previous highwater mark before any incentive fee can be earned.

The performance criteria for the fund manager's incentive fee may incorporate a *hurdle*, which is a minimum performance threshold that the manager must surpass before any fee can be charged to investors. For example, if the hurdle is set at five percent, then the fund valuation must exceed a five percent increase before any incentive fee can be charged.

EXAMPLE

$10 million is invested in a hedge fund. During its first year of operations, the value of this fund declines to $9.5 million. The fund manager will not be able to charge investors an incentive fee until she can return to the fund's value of $10 million.

EXAMPLE

The Hedgehog Fund has $300 million of assets under management. Its fund manager is paid a 1 1/2% management fee on a quarterly basis, on the 10th calendar day of each quarter. Accordingly, the accountant prepares the following entry on April 1 for the April-to-June quarter to accrue the expense:

	Debit	Credit
Prepaid management fees (asset)	$1,125,000	
Accrued management fees (liability)		$1,125,000

On April 10, the accountant pays the management fee to the fund manager, using the following entry:

	Debit	Credit
Accrued management fees (liability)	$1,125,000	
Cash (asset)		$1,125,000

In each month of the quarter, the accountant charges one-third of the prepaid management fees asset to expense, as noted in the following entry for the month of July:

	Debit	Credit
Management fees (expense)	$375,000	
Prepaid management fees (asset)		$375,000

Note: The management fee should be accrued on a daily basis, rather than the monthly basis noted in the preceding example. This day-to-day accrual results in a much more even expense accrual, thereby smoothing out its impact on the daily NAV calculation.

As just indicated, most significant expenses should be accrued on a daily basis, so that there is a consistent daily charge against the NAV. For example, if an insurance provider states a fixed rate for liability insurance, then this can be set up as a daily expense accrual.

Some expenses will be charged by service providers in advance of the related services, while others will be charged in arrears – after the related services have been provided. When the fund pays for expenses in advance, the accountant records them in a prepaid expenses (asset) account, and then charges the amount to expense over the relevant time period. Conversely, when the fund pays for expenses in arrears, the accountant begins to record a daily expense accrual at the start of the coverage period, with the offsetting credit going to an accrued liability account. Then, when the expense is actually paid, the offsetting debit is to the accrued liability account.

EXAMPLE

The Hedgehog Fund pays an annual audit fee of $25,000, paid in arrears. The accountant records an expense accrual for it of $96.15/day (calculated as $25,000 divided by 260 business days), using the following entry:

	Debit	Credit
Audit fees (expense)	$96.15	
Accrued liabilities (liability)		$96.15

At the end of the year, the accountant pays the auditors' bill and records the following entry to clear the accrued liabilities from the fund's books:

	Debit	Credit
Accrued liabilities (liability)	$25,000	
Cash (asset)		$25,000

Bank Accounts

A hedge fund will need at least two bank accounts. One is needed for the ongoing operational expenses of the business, while the other account is used to accept incoming cash from investors and channel money back to them. This separation is needed to avoid commingling cash needed for operational purposes with investor money.

Hedge Fund Reporting

The accountant will be responsible for a standard set of reports and metrics, which will vary somewhat by hedge fund. The most common information reported by a hedge fund includes the amount of assets under management, the operating costs of the fund, the fees earned, and the profit or loss generated by the fund within its latest reporting period.

Summary

The accounting for a hedge fund involves several unique issues not found in other businesses. One is the need to report a net asset value on a daily basis as accurately as possible. Doing so requires that income and expense items be accrued on a daily basis, so that each day's reported NAV reflects an apportionment of these items. Ongoing reconciliations are also needed, to ensure that the reported NAV contains no inaccuracies. And finally, a fund's valuation policy must be rigidly adhered to, thereby ensuring that the fund has a solid basis upon which to report net asset values. In addition, a hedge fund may need to employ side pocket accounts to deal with illiquid assets (depending on the nature of the assets acquired) and capital accounts (if the entity is structured as a partnership). These issues present unique challenges for the accountant.

Glossary

A

Absolute return strategy. The concept of always seeking a positive return on investment, irrespective of market conditions.

Aggregate method. When all realized profits and losses are netted for a period and then allocated to partners.

B

Bond. A fixed obligation to pay that is issued by a corporation or government entity to investors.

E

Ex-dividend date. The date on which it is determined who will receive a company's dividend.

H

Hedge fund. An investment partnership that uses pooled funds and applies a variety of aggressive investment strategies to a wide range of financial products in order to earn returns for its investors.

High-water mark. The fund value baseline from which gains are calculated – and from which a fund manager's incentive fee is derived.

Hurdle. A minimum performance threshold that a fund manager must surpass before any fee can be charged to investors.

L

Layering method. When profits and losses are allocated to partner accounts as of the date when they are realized.

M

Mark to market. Adjusting the value of an asset to reflect its value as determined by current market conditions.

N

Net asset value. The net value of a fund, which is calculated as the total value of its assets minus the total value of its liabilities.

R

Redemption. The withdrawal of funds from a hedge fund by an investor.

S

Side pocket. An account that a hedge fund uses to segregate riskier or illiquid assets from the rest of its investments.

Subscription. A payment by an investor into a hedge fund.

T

Trade claim. An unsecured obligation of a debtor that has filed for bankruptcy protection, which is held by a creditor.

Trade date. The date when an order related to a security is executed in the market.

Index

www.ingramcontent.com/pod-product-compliance
Lightning Source LLC
Chambersburg PA
CBHW051431200326
41520CB00023B/7433